D1571355

A Sprig of Holly

HALFORD E. LUCCOCK

Charles S. Hartman, EDITOR

The Pilgrim Press

New York • Philadelphia

Copyright © 1978 The Pilgrim Press

Acknowledgments appear on pages 63-64.

Library of Congress Cataloging in Publication Data

Luccock, Halford Edwards, 1885-1960.
  A sprig of holly.

  1. Christmas—Meditations.   I. Hartman,
Charles S., 1913-   II. Title.
BV45.L74   242′.33   78-17096
ISBN 0-8298-0354-8

The Pilgrim Press, 287 Park Avenue South, New York, New York 10010

Contents

Preface

Here is a collection of Christmas writings of Halford E. Luccock. To those of us who knew him, we will hear again the dry wit and the penetrating and challenging sound of his beloved voice speaking through the words. To those of you who are here finding him for the first time, you are in for one of those delightful and wonderful surprises that Christmas can bring!

I am pleased to share these Christmas insights of Dr. Luccock, who was my teacher and my friend. The three years I spent in his stimulating classes at Yale Divinity School were just the beginning. The voice I heard in the classroom and the chapel continued to speak to me in following years, not only in friendly correspondence but also through the person of Simeon Stylites and other writings.

I filled several scrapbooks with the Simeon Stylites columns, placing the Christmas pieces together in one section. I enjoyed and cherished all of them, but the Christmas letters were my favorites. At Christmastime I shared them with friends. Why not, I thought, seek to have these published, so they can bring joy to many more people and add a sparkle to their Christmas.

So, to all of us, may this little book bring his cheerful "Merry Christmas" greetings, with his peculiarly colorful sprig of holly to decorate the season with joyful chuckles and poignant insights.

Charles S. Hartman

Christmas
Is Most Irregular

A Partridge in a
Pear Tree

With Christmas coming up, may I remind you that there is no carol that offers more fun for a few people singing together, whether they can sing or not, than the old standby "The Twelve Days of Christmas." There is a fine lilt to it, and the fascination that children of all ages find in a cumulative song on the model of "The House that Jack Built," where the list of things to be remembered and repeated gets longer with each stanza and you get all out of breath and have a grand time.

It is an old and universal carol, in celebration of the twelve days from Christmas to Epiphany. You know it—

> On the first day of Christmas
> My true love gave to me
> A partridge in a pear tree.

Then it goes on with a list of the most riotously inappropriate and ludicrous gifts—two turtle doves, three French hens, six geese laying, seven swans swimming, eight maids milking, ending with twelve drummers drumming.

8

Nonsense? Not by a jugful of wassail. It is a profound philosophy of giving. It celebrates the high wisdom of completely inappropriate and largely useless gifts. And a good thing to remember just before Christmas. A partridge in a pear tree—what on earth could one do with that? That's the beauty of it! That makes it something to sing about! And folks have been singing about it for several hundred years. Would they have sung about a floor mop (highly appropriate for housecleaning) or a teakettle or a foot-warmer? Not much!

So take a suggestion for your shopping list. Give your true love an inappropriate gift. Don't get grandma another lace cap or pair of woolen mittens. She has plenty already, and besides she hates the things. Get her a little bottle of Chanel No. 5 or a set of lipsticks or a pair of dancing slippers. That will boost her morale, make her feel she is still alive. As you reach for that fine book for your beloved pastor, the learned tome *Archaeology and the Bible,* stay your hand. Reach over to the next counter and get him the *New Yorker Book of Cartoons.* There will be several cartoons by Peter Arno, highly inappropriate for the clergy. That's the idea. There are few joys greater than that of stepping out of character for a time. And I'll bet it will do a lot more for the sermons too. And father—lay off the neckties and the conservative scarf. Get him a Lionel electric train, appropriate for age nine. (All his own; children keep away!) Dad has always had a yen for one. And for your husband or wife—well, that has me stumped, as usual. How about a—er—ah—Oh well, how about a partridge in a pear tree? It would be a surprise.

The best gifts of love are those which show a lovely

lack of common sense. Flowers (they fade, don't they?), a bracelet (invariably a nuisance). It is usually on the twenty-fifth anniversary that a husband gives a vacuum cleaner or a mixmaster.

There is high precedent for all this. The first Christmas gift was highly inappropriate—a baby in a barn. Who wanted that? No one clapped and said, "Goody, goody, just what I wanted!" That is, no one except a few souls who could really see—Simeon and Anna in the Temple, some shepherds, His mother.

> They were all looking for a king
> To slay their foes and lift them high.
> Thou cam'st a little baby thing
> To make a woman cry.*

A sprig of holly to you!

---

*From "That Holy Thing" by George Macdonald.

Whoops! It's Christmas!

Whoops! It's Christmas, in which the old order of seating changeth. The other day I bumped into Santa Claus. A good bump it was, too! I ought to have been arrested, for there is no open season on Santa Claus. But sometimes a first-class collision is an exciting thing. It will knock the wind out of you, and it may knock an idea into your head. True, this Santa Claus did not have white cotton whiskers or a red coat, but she was the real thing all right! Santa Claus in the flesh and plenty of it.

A lady, who looked like an animated Christmas tree with packages dangling from every limb, and I bumped and spilled. As I was trying to pick up the packages she gasped out, "Oh, I hate Christmas, anyhow! It turns everything upside down."

I said, "That is just what it was made for." But this lofty sentiment did not stop her dirty looks at all. But it *is* the big thing about Christmas!

Christmas is a story about a baby, and that is a baby's chief business, turning things upside down. It is gross slander on babies that their chief passion is food. It is rearrangement! Every orthodox baby rearranges everything he or she sees, or can get his or her little hooks into, from the order of who's important in the family, to the dishes on the table. A baby in a family

11

divides time into two eras, just as Christmas does. There is B.C., which means "before child," and A.D., which means "after deluge."

The central core of truth is that Christmas turns everything upside down, the upside of heaven come down to earth. The Christmas story puts a new value on every person. A person is not a thing to be used, not a chemical accident, not an educated ape. Everyone is a VIP, because he or she has divine worth. That was revealed when "Love came down at Christmas." A scientist said, making a plea for exchange scholarships between nations, "The best way to send an idea is to wrap it up in a person." That was what happened at Christmas. The idea of divine love was wrapped up in a person.

Christmas is good news in a world of bad news. This was so on the first Christmas and on every Christmas. During the blackout of London in the Second World War, a newspaper correspondent wrote, "The night was so dark that even the cats ran into each other." That *would* be a dark night! We are often tempted today to think that of our world. But Christmas brings hope in a dark world.

Christmas puts down the mighty things in a person's mind, such as place, rights, power, and exalts the things of low degree, humility, simplicity, and trust. Charles Lamb set high praise on All Fools' Day. He wrote, "All Fools' Day says to people, 'You look wise; pray correct that error.'" Christmas says to each of us, "You look great; pray correct that error."

Christmas turns things inside out, and under the spell of the Christmas story the locked-up treasures of kindliness and sympathy come from the inside of the heart to the outside world of actual deed. The danger that we all run is that when we keep the kindness locked inside, our biography can be written in one sentence: "This little pig went to market." The symbol of Christmas is a gift.

And Christmas turns things tail-end foremost. The day and the spirit of Christmas rearrange the world parade. As the world arranges it, usually there come first in importance—leading the parade with a big blare of a band—the Big Shots. Frequently they are also the Stuffed Shirts. That's the first of the parade. Then at the tail end, as of little importance, trudge the weary, the poor, the lame, the halt, and the blind. But in the Christmas spirit the procession is turned around. Those at the tail end are put first in the arrangement of the Child of Christmas.

Christmas calls for haste to meet the world's need. In the Christmas story in Luke we read how the shepherds "came with haste." Evidently the Christmas rush started early! The first response to the good news was speed, hurry, haste, rush. We have a different kind of Christmas rush. Masefield's line "Life's a long headache in a noisy street" was not written about Christmas but it is a fair description of the shopping rush. One of the ironies of our time is that the celebration of Christmas has become the most frantic convulsion of commercialism. In many places the loudest Christmas bell is the one attached to the cash register. For a few days before Christmas we sing, "God rest ye merry, gentle folk," but there is little rest. We sing, "Silent night, holy night . . . sleep

13

in heavenly peace," but there is little peace. There is, however, a real rush in which we should join to bring peace and help to a needy world.

We need a new arrangement of the human parade which passes before our eyes. Here is the order of seating in an old New England church: "First, dignity of descent; Second, place of public office; Third, pious disposition; Fourth, estate; Last, peculiar serviceableness of any kind." Christmas comes along and knocks that arrangement into a cocked hat. Yet often we unconsciously arrange our acquaintances, or possible acquaintances, in the order of what advantage they may be to us. That scheme belongs on the junk pile! "The last shall be first."

Let old man Scrooge have the last word. At the end of his travels, which were started by the ghost of Jacob Marley, who "was dead to begin with," after giving his years to what he thought was his business he discovered this: "Humankind was my business. Human need was my business." A good idea to bump into!

So, deck the halls with holly!

Christmas Roses

There they are. There is no doubt about it. Incredible, but true. Christmas roses, blooming in a bed of snow! Ever-green leaves and ever-blooming flowers—white, shaped like a wild rose. People going by stop and gaze with wide-eyed astonishment. The roses have absolutely no business to be there! But they are no optical illusion. Astonishing!

That astonishment of people stopped on the side-walk is a symbol of one of the great gifts of Christmas: its quickening of the capacity for astonishment. That is a gift desperately needed in a world where the capacity for amazement is becoming more and more depleted. The decline of the ability to wonder, to be astonished, is partly the result of the tragedy of growing up, of losing much of that rich fund of curiosity with which the child is endowed.

A.A. Milne pictured alluringly the child's inheritance of wonder when he wrote of a boy's reeling off a list of amazing things he could see while out for a walk: sun on river and hill; the sound of the sea "if you stand quite still"; new puppies at a nearby farm; most awe-inspiring of all, an old sailor with an empty sleeve. But—there were the grown-ups standing quite still instead of jumping with joy, able only to admonish: "Run along, run along."

15

Oldsters can so easily become a Society for the Suppression of Astonishment. The vision splendid in the child's eye so often fades into the light of very common day. So it is fitting that Christmas, the festival of the Child, should bring the gift of astonishment restored.

The Christmas story began with wonder. The shepherds were "sore afraid." That is, they were stunned with astonishment. The whole affair was fantastic. Chesterton sensed the very genius of the day: "the things that cannot be and were."

And how sorely we need an increased ability to wonder! Ours is a world surfeited with facts and information and entertainment, but deficient in wonder. We have an unceasing parade of novelties, but a "rapidity of things going stale." It is one of the strange paradoxes of our time that a world full of wonders has lost the sense of wonder. The two are quite different. We gape at a bewildering succession of marvelous machines, but there is little of the deep amazement felt on the Judean hills so long ago: "When I consider the heavens, the work of thy fingers, the moon and the stars which thou hast ordained." One reason religion to so many becomes flat, stale, and wearisome is that the sheer wonder is left out.

Increasingly we live in a pushbutton world: no surprises, no fantastic wonders; just common sense, which gets to be as stale as the "remainder biscuit after a voyage." But Christmas knocks a routine world of order topsy-turvy. Everything is gloriously out of place: a song in the sky, a baby in a barn. That out-of-placeness brings astonishment to lives needing badly the thrill of wonder. For life is truly measured not by the number of breaths taken, but by the number not taken, the occasions when

16

breath is stopped in amazement. This is the breathtaking astonishment of Christmas.

Christmas roses—a root out of dry ground, the Dayspring from on high—that is enough astonishment for one day, and for all the days.

And many of them to you.

Irregular

The hymnals I like best are those which have little musical directions at the top of the page, indicating how the hymn should be played and sung. Not that it makes much vocal difference to me. I cannot aspire to fulfilling the injunction to "make a *joyful* noise unto the Lord"; it is all pretty doleful. But I can obey the command, in the 98th psalm, "Make a *loud* noise and rejoice."

Just the same, the musical directions enliven your thoughts. I have always been startled by the musical direction which goes with the hymn "Onward, Christian Soldiers"—"May be sung in unison." Exactly! It had *better* be sung in unison! The loveliest one of all is the direction which goes with the Christmas carol "There's a song in the air, There's a star in the sky." The direction reads, "Irregular." I should say so! The whole thing was highly irregular! A baby in a barn. What could be more irregular than that? Shockingly irregular!

Two thoughts, decked with holly for Christmas, come out of this musical notation. We have in Christianity a most irregular religion. We worship a most irregular God, whose ways are past finding out. Anything can happen. The worst enemies of vital Christianity are those who have tried to regularize it, to take out its fantastic, peculiar qualities and leave it no different from anything else. Thus, often, a company called to be disturbers have dwindled down into a company of regular folks, achieving the fine regularity of the cemetery.

Here's the other thought—a baby in a barn! There was a place in the organized life of Judea in which babies might be born. It was not a barn. But there was no room in the inn, so a barn was used. God never gets to the end of the rope. If there is no room in the fitting place, God uses another, even a manger.

There is a place for every new revelation of God to be born. That place is God's church. But if there is no room in the church—as there has often been no room— God can find a barn or other place in which God's new word can be born.

There was a time in the early nineteenth century for a new revelation of the meaning of the Christian gospel. That was while the slaughter of the innocents was going on, a slaughter of children, often mere babies, in mine and factory, which made Herod's little exploit in killing look like pretty small stuff. When the Ten Hours bill, limiting the labor of children to ten hours a day, was introduced in Parliament the bishops of the Church of England, who had seats in the House of Lords, voted overwhelmingly against it. You can see the godly bishops, "goodly in girth," protesting fervently against the weak sentimentalism of allowing the children of the poor to get off with a mere ten hours a day at work.

There was no room in the inn of the church, so that baby was born in a barn. There were of course individual Christians, such as Shaftesbury, who led in the fight. But the new insight into the rights of childhood came from

19

labor rather than in the institution where such new insights might be expected to originate.

The inn was full, but that did not stop the incarnation. There is need for new revelations of the meaning of the Christian message. Will they come in the church or in a barn?

Christmas
Is Light Shining
into Our Darkness

Christmas Meditation

(In a Department Store)

A strange medley of noise fell on my ears in Aisle C, Main Floor, of the Megalopolitan Department Store. The Caroleers, perched precariously on a platform near the elevator shaft, were bravely fighting a losing battle to lift the strains of "Holy Night" above the babel that rose from the counters.

"Going UP! Room for six more. Don't push!" . . . "No, madam, hair brushes cannot be exchanged." . . . "The complaint department is on the third floor." . . . "Above thy deep and dreamless sleep." . . . "I think a silver cocktail shaker would have a nice Christmasy feeling, don't you?" . . . "Something in a simple apron. Ah—Er—It's for my maid." . . . "I don't want to give them anything, but I suppose I have to. But not over four dollars." . . . "Repeat the sounding joy." . . .

Christmas gifts—to the merry chime of the cash register! The mood of Keith Preston's immortal lines celebrating an uncommercialized Christmas—the First Christmas—came to mind:

> Peter was a fisher boy
> Helping with the haul;
> Pilate was a shavetail

Leading troops in Gaul.
Judas was as innocent
As little child can be;
The wood that made the crucifix
Was still a growing tree;
Unminted was the silver
That made the traitor's pay;
And none had yet commercialized
The spirit of the day.*

While waiting for my change, I thought of how the first Christmas gifts, the gold, frankincense, and myrrh of the wise men, would have looked if they had been given in the spirit and with the motive of much of the frenzied Christmas giving and shopping that marks our annual yuletide orgy. If they had followed a very common modern pattern, that first Christmas might have been something like this:

Caspar whispers to Melchior: "I suppose we really have to take something out to Bethlehem. Especially since I feel sure that Balthazar will make his usual splurge. He has gold, you know, and that will outshine everyone else. I'm going to give some frankincense. I always say it is the spirit that counts and not the price. Besides, I found some at a little place, so much cheaper than at the bazaar."

Melchior replies: "I believe in practical gifts myself. I have some myrrh with me, and I am going to give that. Besides, we don't know how important these people

---

really are. Is it reasonable to look for David's line in a stable? Herod had doubts about it, you remember."

Balthazar says to himself: "It is worthwhile giving gold. That will make Caspar and Melchior look pretty small. More than that, there may be quite a lot of publicity about this baby, and it won't do any harm to make a good showing."

But perhaps they did not do it that way at all. "And they came into the house and saw the young child with Mary his mother; and they fell down and worshiped him; and opening their treasures they offered unto him gifts, gold and frankincense and myrrh."

I feel distinct symptoms of a "moral" coming on, so I had better hastily subscribe myself.

A border of holly to you!

The First Noel—
As It Might Have Been!

As we go about the Christmas commercial orgy and as each day gets more tense—"only X more shopping days till Christmas"—our thoughts go back to the first Christmas. How much more might have been made out of that Christmas if that simple time had known the means and methods and aims which modern advances have brought to our more enlightened days. With our nuclear-age techniques they could have made a really Big Thing out of Christmas. What a success it could have been!

Just think what a terrific opportunity the first Noel would have offered to television. They could have had the angel's song from the sky on an All-Judean Hookup. That would have been a spectacular beyond any triumph of all the networks today. And think of the possible interviews with shepherds on a Person-to-Person program, the wonders that could have been done with the visit of the wise men! What a parade could have been videoed, complete with camels and gorgeously costumed kings—all beyond anything that Barnum and Bailey and Ringling ever dreamed of. And the manger scene in a well-equipped modern barn (furnishings by International Harvester)—followed by a sequence in the Grand Ballroom of the Bethlehem Inn, Incorporated, scene of the crowning of Miss Noel of year zero, attended by a bevy of runner-up beauties. (A rigged contest, you ask? Who cares?)

The greatest loss in the whole simple affair was, of course, the fact that nobody made any money out of it at all. No sponsors, no advertisers, no record-breaking sales! That, in light of our modern improvements on Christmas, was the greatest failure. No merry little Christmas bells ringing up sales on a cash register (the merriest Christmas bells that many people ever hear today). No lovely carol such as "Silent Night, Holy Night" played in bedecked stores against a background of the most unholy noise that frenzied sales commotion ever concocted. Think of what advances on that simple affair there might have been by our modern advertising and sales miracles. What a market for little mangers of gold, silver, and plastic! How robes for the well-dressed person, patterned after those of the wise men, would have swept the country!

Foolish? Of course. But not more foolish than the improvements which modern "magic" has added to Christmas celebrations, in which the manipulators seem to know no more of what Christmas is all about than did the innkeeper that first Noel. For the nativity was not an event in a salesperson's paradise but in the mind and heart of God.

May words come through the Christmas turmoil saying, "Let us go even now unto Bethlehem." Even now. A journey to a knowledge of what it is all about. A few years ago a woman came to a minister with a hard prob-

26

lem; she said that she was chairperson of a Community Christmas Tree Celebration and was having terrible difficulty selecting the songs for it—the Christmas carols were all "so distressingly theological." The minister said, "Well, Christmas was a rather theological affair, wasn't it?" It was not something about record sales but something about the universe and its God. A highly theological affair!

So—God rest you merry, gentle folk.

Take Plato Christmas
Shopping with You

What makes me sure that Plato will be a good companion on a Christmas shopping trip is his record of a stroll
through the marketplace at Athens. This record is not in
one of his dialogues but in a monologue. At any rate, he
reported, "I love to walk through the marketplace and
see the things on sale. It makes me happy to see so many
things I do not want."

So, you see, he would be an ideal companion! And
the days before Christmas are an ideal time for rejoicing
gaily over the infinite variety of things you do not want,
including many things, very expensive, which no one but
a stark imbecile could want.

Let me add to your Christmas joy with a few notes
on a stroll which I took—not along Market Street; I am
too lazy for that—but through the advertising pages of
two slick paper magazines, the *New Yorker* and *Vogue*
for December. It was a profitable trip, for I saved about
$18,000 by not wanting a dozen pieces of junk which
were offered. If you want to save some money, come
along.

Abercrombie & Fitch offer a Brandy Stick, "a sturdy unbreakable cane with a real hollow leg that carries its own brandy flask for sudden crisis." Mark Cross will sell you for $71 (tax included), "just the present for daddy," a "home bartender set," including "a double jigger, an automatic corkscrew, and bottle opener." Think of it, only $71!

Then, my heart rejoiced at the Oriental Sleeping Pajamas offered by Sulka, at only $67.50.

> O sleep, it is a gentle thing,
> Beloved from pole to pole—*

but not at that price! The $67.50 would keep me awake all night. How about a Tiffany Clip Brooch at $14,850? Think of what I save by not wanting to be clipped! Ah, here is just what I don't want— a Resistol Felt Hat, Number 100, at $100. What a crown for a bald head! No, thank you! Then I rejoice in the suspenders which I don't want for $8.50. It's a holdup! I can get a hand-wrought bar for only $90 from the Gallo Furniture Company. It will take the place of the bookcase in the living room.

Here is the prize, the perfect gift—I almost felt a twinge of longing, but I stoutly resisted, though it was a hard fight. For the perfect gift was a gold toothpick for $25 including tax. You will probably want one, so I give you the address: The Golden Man, San Francisco. I give all these addresses to prove that I am not spinning a fantastic fairy tale, but can give you the precise page

---

*From *The Rime of the Ancient Mariner* by Samuel Taylor Coleridge.

number for each item, telling you the truth, the whole truth, and the silliest truth that ever got into print, says I. Oh, yes, and I must not forget the little flamingo pin, a nice thing for the suit, fresh-water pearl, just $2,400.

I could go on for 200 pages and $30,000 more, but you get the idea. You have already saved $18,000, if you feel the same as I do. I hope I have brightened the day for you.

The same to you.

Wise Men from the West

I heard the words being read, "In the days of Herod the king, behold, wise men from the East came to Jerusalem . . ." Then my mind, never very strong at sticking to the point, trailed off. Suppose, I thought, suppose that the wise men had come from the West rather than from the East. Suppose, too, that they shared and expressed some of the main, dominant ideas and drives of our Western civilization and world. What would have happened if it had been wise men from the West journeying eastward toward a star? The extracanonical scriptures might have read like this:

The first wise man, being a top ruler in the Western world, was a merchant prince, a big industrialist, ever alert to the opportunity to bigger and better sales. At the start of the journey he said to himself: "We are going to be traveling through large, untapped markets. I can follow the star and at the same time open up new outlets for the Caspar Manufacturing Company and triple our exports." So he diligently called on all the tradespeople along the way. He amassed a big sheaf of orders. But it all took time and delayed him greatly, so that the star faded and he never got to Bethlehem at all.

The second wise man had a true Western feeling for military power and defense. He said to himself: "We will be traveling through foreign nations and strange peoples.

31

The gifts we bear will need armed protection. I must recruit a strong force and arm them well. Otherwise we will never get to Jerusalem." But the recruiting and problems of logistics took time, and his soldiers were always getting into brawls with the soldiers of the nations through which they passed. Rome refused to allow such a menacing task force to pass through Italy. So they did not get any farther than Gaul, where they went into winter quarters.

The third wise man was very different from the other two, in everything except his vision of the star and the desire to find the king. But he too was a true man of Western culture and aims. He had been called many harsh things by rivals, but no one had ever called him a shrinking violet. He had a high position—no less than president of Melchior, Melchior, Melchior & Melchior, Advertising and Public Relations Consultants. He said to himself: "This finding of a new king will be a tremendously big thing. It has great publicity possibilities and must be handled in a big way. We will be marching right into history and the whole world must get the full story." So he was much engaged in giving out press releases at every town at which they stopped, and entertaining local journalists. For the sake of complete coverage he made a detour into Egypt, which took three months. But by that time the king of the Jews had been born at Bethlehem, and he never got to see the king at all or to present his gifts.

Perhaps it is just as well that the wise men came from the East. Perhaps the West, with all its power and skill, still misses the way to the star and the babe in swaddling clothes.

An Unsegregated Christmas

Charles Williams of England, who was one of the gen-
uine mystics of our time and also a great novelist and
poet, has given us in his poem "The Epiphany" a mem-
orable picture of an unsegregated Christmas. It fits a time
of conflict over color and race. Williams pictures the wise
men coming to the Child:

> It was a king of Negro-land,
>   A king of China-town,
> And an old prince of Iran,
>   Who to the Child kneeled down.
>
> It was a king of blackamoors,
>   A king of men slant-eyed,
> A lord among sun-worshippers,
>   Who at the New-born spied.
>
> It was a king with savage eyes,
>   King with a queer pigtail,
> King with a high and sunlit brow,
>   Who bade the New-born "Hail!"

Back rode they to one country,
   One spiritual land,
Three kings of my soul's country
   Who touched the New-born's hand.*

God's Rainbow of All Colors! This would fit the
Christmas decorations of Norfolk, of Cape Town, of Little
Rock, of all the world's cities crowded with folk of many
colors and nations.

The wise men are not only a symbol of the universal
truth of Christmas; they are a prophecy of the coming of
varied peoples into one country. And just as the kings of
diverse colors and races found a leering opposition to
their gathering at the manger, so there are obstacles set
up by die-hards who fight against an unsegregated
Christmas in school, in church. Walter Bagehot said of
King George III of England that for most of his life he
was a "consecrated obstruction." There are some such
in our churches—"consecrated obstructions" to the re-
alization of the one family of God and of one class of
American citizens. Many of them have inherited their
sacred prejudices, and are sworn to keep them unspoiled
by any examination in the light of present realities.

H.G. Wells wrote of his mother that "she went to
a finishing school and at the age of nineteen she was
finished." "Ideas," he said, "rattled around in her head
like bullets in an empty container. You could hear the
hard little bullets rattle around, ideas that were shaped
thirty years ago." So in the fight for an unsegregated

---

*Charles Williams, "The Epiphany," *Poems of Conformity*.

world, you can hear the little bullets rattle around in certain heads.

Charles Williams' poem is a work of fancy, a putting into verse of the one family of God, with the unspeakable gift of equal justice.

> It was a king with savage eyes,
>   King with a queer pigtail,
> King with a high and sunlit brow,
>   Who bade the New-born "Hail!"

Christmas Is Not a Stopping Place

Get Christmas
Out of the Stocking

A number of years ago Gerald Stanley Lee wrote some words about Christmas which are always in order. His plea was to keep Christmas to its original size. Here was the original size of Christmas: "Behold, I bring you good tidings of great joy, *which shall be to all people*." It was for *all people*—it was Christmas Unlimited. Mr. Lee put it in this arresting way:

Why should Christmas—that stern, imperious moment in the world when with a child's cry and a woman's smile, God turned the world over, and began all in a minute a new human race—why should Christmas be tucked away in people's minds as a feebly pretty country sentiment, a woman's holiday, a baby's frolic, the sublimest event on earth thrust playfully into the bottom of a stocking?

There is danger that the very loveliness of Christmas as a home festival may imprison it within the home, and thus people may forget that it is a *world* festival, celebrating the truth that God so loved the world—all of it—that God gave the only begotten son. Christmas must be pulled out of a stocking and carried to the dispossessed, the defrauded, to the whole globe, as well as to America.

Jesus deliberately widened the family ties to include the kinship of all humankind. "Whosoever shall do the will of God, the same is my brother, and my sister, and my mother [Mark 3:33-34]."

The danger of living in too small a world is a danger that Christmas ought to overcome.

Christmas Day
in the Morning

Of all the Christmas celebrations I ever heard of, two stick like burrs in my memory. No carols, no holly, no Christmas trees or sleigh bells. But Christmas parties just the same.

The first was on Christmas morning 1809, at Danville, Kentucky, on the edge of the wilderness. A young physician, Ephraim McDowell, who had come into Kentucky only two jumps behind Daniel Boone, was preparing for a surgical operation in which he not only risked the life of his patient but also took his own life in his hands. Mrs. Thomas Crawford had made an agonizing journey of sixty miles on horseback to see if her life could be saved. To save her required an abdominal operation of a sort that had never before been performed in all medical history. It meant cutting into the abdominal cavity, which then, all over the world, was labeled plain murder. Yet this backwoods doctor, his only equipment a plain wooden table, on which the patient was strapped, stood ready to do what no one had ever dared before.

Outside the house an angry mob had gathered and thrown a rope over a limb of a tree, ready to hang Dr.

McDowell if the patient died. But he counted not life dear unto himself. He went ahead, and the patient lived. That operation was the forerunner of a major part of modern surgery. James Thomas Flexner says, "Every operation for appendicitis or gall stones since is a lineal descendent of one daring experiment in the wilderness of Kentucky." A Christmas gift!

Drop down the calendar about a hundred years, to 1900. It is now Christmas Day in the morning in Santiago, Cuba. There a private soldier in the United States army, John J. Moran (a name that deserves more remembrance than it has received), celebrated Christmas by coming down with a whopping case of yellow fever, every symptom perfect. Yellow fever did not just happen to Private Moran; he asked for it. He offered his life as a test of the theory which Dr. Walter Reed and others were working on, that yellow fever was transmitted by mosquitoes. Four days earlier Moran had entered a closed room and voluntarily played host to a swarm of mosquitoes that had been feasting on yellow-fever patients. Early on Christmas morning he entered the valley of the shadow of death. After a long seige he recovered, and brought back with him the indisputable proof of the cause of yellow fever—the truth that has practically wiped yellow fever off the map of the world.

Not very Christmasy stories, these. No atmosphere, no off-stage music. Or was there music? Perhaps the herald angels did sing. At any rate, these are stories of a fitting celebration of the birthday of One who came to give his life a ransom for many.

The same to you and many of them!

The Baby Grew Up

The Christmas story is the story of a baby. That is a part of its inexhaustible pull on the mind and heart of humanity. But it is also a liability. For a great many people become so entranced with the beautiful story of a baby in a manger that they miss the chief point of the story, and hence do not feel the compulsion which it lays on life. We can become so charmed with the story of a baby that we grow sentimental about it; it does not ask that we do anything about it; it does not demand any vital change in our way of thinking and living.

But the chief point of the story is that *the baby grew up!* He grew up to become the sternest challenge to a world of hard power that had ever been made. He was no sentimentalist; he was a terrible realist! Everything opposed to love and unity in our world, he declared flatly, is doomed and damned—for the reason that at the center of the universe is a God of loving purpose to all people.

The great question for us is this: Is our Christmas still only a story about a baby, or is it more, a deathless story about a Person into whom the baby grew, who can redeem the world from its sins, and who calls us into partnership with his great and mighty purposes?

42

Let's Give Seven Yells!

One of the quaint bits of lore connected with the Christmas celebration is part of the history of the churches of twelfth-century Paris. There, on Christmas Sunday, the "people of low degree" filled the churches, rubbing shoulders with their "betters," the feudal aristocracy. When in the course of the service, the Magnificat was read and the stirring words were pronounced, "He hath put down the mighty from their seats, and exalted them of low degree," the folk "of low degree," recognizing their cue, would yell their heads off in approval, with a noise that almost lifted the roof. For long years this chaos reigned unconfined. Then in 1198 the bishop of Paris decreed that after seven yells—that medieval form of Amen—the clamor must stop. So thereafter the plain people had to content themselves with giving to the program of "exalting them of low degree" only seven rounds of applause.

Seven is really a holy number. Today the cause of true democracy rates seven good lusty yells. And that is seven times more than it is getting in some places in this "home of the free" at the present time.

The folk "of low degree" in medieval Paris had a sure insight in recognizing that the Magnificat is a charter for kinship and the valuation of humankind at a high rate. That same insight was expressed by Quentin Reynolds when he said: "If I were a dictator the first book I would burn would be the Bible. I'd burn it because I'd recognize that the whole concept of democracy came out of that book. The Greeks had a word for it, but the Bible gave us the philosophy for the way of life."

Since seven yells are allowed by episcopal permission, how about giving them now? The cause of the worth of individuals, of people as human beings and children of God, is hard beset in this land. It could stand seven yells loud enough to be heard [all over the world] where the cause of people as human beings and as first-class citizens is taking a severe drubbing.

As we look over the news from foreign lands and reflect on some parts of the United States' foreign policy in recent years, we feel deeply, and often with shame, the need of full-throated yells for freedom, for democracy, for the Magnificat—that is, for the peoples of the earth, the oppressed, the burdened. Our country began in revolution, in rebellion against colonialism. Why can't we live up to our past, and not give to other countries the strong suspicion that we are ashamed of it? Why must we line up on the side of the dictatorships? That alignment hasn't been of much help to us.

A real yell for democracy would startle the world. So all together, one, two, three!

*Christmas
Is Music
in the Key of Hope*

Living on Tiptoe

She . . . gave thanks to God and spoke about the child
to all who were *living in expectation* of the liberation of
Jerusalem.—*Luke 2:38*

A fine way to live—expectation of liberation!

There existed a definite class of people in the Israel
of Jesus' day consisting of sentinel souls who lived in the
expectation that something was going to happen. And
the very expectation that God would do something
helped immeasurably to make it happen. For that group
of people were the seed plot in which Jesus' message
first took root. They received him because they were
looking for him.

It is such sentinel souls who make possible the liberation of humankind from the grip of ancient wrong.
Nothing really great ever happened without a great many
lives being lived "in expectation." Arthur J. Gossip in
The Galilean Accent says finely:

They are the kind of folks by whom the world moves forward:
who live in a *qui vive* of expectancy, always standing on tiptoe,
always sure that something big may happen at any time. Hush!
Is not this it coming now? With people like that God can do
anything. But you and I keep thwarting [God] by sheer dullness
of spirit. We are listless, apathetic, blasé, bored; our hopes are
small and thin. There is no audacity in our expectation.

46

Lorne Pierce traces the same truth back to the Old Testament:

A.B. Davidson once called the prophets "always terribly one-sided people." That single idea was that "God is going to do something." "God is surely coming!" cried Isaiah. "[God] is here, at our very door!" answers Zephaniah. And so each and every one by their faith made it possible, yea, certain, for some great spiritual surprise to take place. It is upon this that the rest is builded: "And when the time was fulfilled—Jesus came." Did it ever happen otherwise? Truth is [a ruler] that only comes to visit subjects along the highway of great longing. Science advances to its kingdom along the avenues of expectancy. Religion comes into its own along the road of loving hearts, that great-hearted clan of intrepid believers.*

But not all of Christ's followers feel this quickened pulse beat of expectant faith.

Some are *asleep*.

Some are *satisfied*. Their eyes never wistfully scan the horizon. Their hearts are never hungry.

Some are looking but they are *looking back*. The golden age for them is in the past. For some reason yesterday belonged to God but not tomorrow. They say good-bye to sunsets but never welcome a dawn.

There is an even deeper meaning in the words "living in expectation" than appears on the surface. It is this: only as we live in expectation do we truly live at all.

Are our spirits on tiptoe or stretched on a couch? There is one easy way to learn the answer. What is our

---

*From *In Conference with the Best Minds*. Used by permission of Abingdon Press.

habitual attitude to the world's "impossibles," to the great dreams of humanity—the abolition of war, the coming of the unity of all humankind, the curbing of greed, the exploitation of the unprivileged? Do we live, and work, in eager expectation of these things?

"She'll Be Comin' Round the Mountain"

A crowd of youngsters in a church parlor were having a Christmas "sing" around a briskly burning fire on the hearth. One lad with a lovely whisky tenor started the old song "She'll Be Comin' Round the Mountain When She Comes." The leader was shocked. "No, no!" she cried. "That is *not* a Christmas carol." And all melody stopped short.

But one observer, all set to burst into barbershop chords, thought: "You're all wrong, sister! That emphatically *is* a Christmas carol, and a good one." For "she'll be comin' round the mountain when she comes" is a forecast of hope, in a world where hope is in very short supply. It is the business of Christmas to bring hope. It began that way—"to give light to them that sit in darkness and in the shadow of death." And that is right where we sit today, "in the shadow of death."

We are in a mountain country. If there is to be any real hope for the world, think of the mountains we must get around. Mountains of prejudice that loom like Ever-

49

est, mountains of ignorance, of ancestral blindness, of entrenched privilege, of inertia, which block the road to a better world like a range of the Rockies.

So the news that "she'll be comin' round the mountain" is "good news which shall be to all people." This is not only hope; it is history. For a "great day coming" *has* come around great mountains. Think of the power of the slave trade in England in the eighteenth century. *There* was a mountain that sat on top of trade, of government, and, yes, of the church. But change did come around it.

We read in the letter to the Corinthians of "faith to remove mountains." But if the mountains of evil don't move—and a lot of them seem to be set pretty solidly— we can come around them. There are mountains that we cannot blast away or tunnel through. Christmas hope and faith sings that "she'll be comin' round the mountains" that block the way.

Thus Christmas saves us from the ultimate despair, such as that of the dying H.G. Wells, who wrote in his last years: "It now seems to me that the whole universe is utterly bored by the whole species of mankind. I can see the human race sweeping along the stream of fate to defeat, degradation and final defeat." That seems to cover it! No program ahead except that of Richard II:

> For God's sake, let us sit upon the ground
> And tell sad stories of the death of kings.

There is another line of action. We can all rise and instead of intoning that dirge we can sing a different tune: Christ "shall reign forever and ever."

We are told that Christmas is this and Christmas is that. As a matter of fact Christmas is a whistle, proclaiming that something is coming round the mountain. It may be away off, but it'll be comin', sure. So get up on tiptoe and listen. Can't you hear it? There it is: "The dayspring from on high hath visited us. . . . And thou, Child, shalt go before the face of the Lord to prepare his ways, and . . . guide our feet into the way of peace."

So deck the halls with holly!

H.G. Wells
Meets the Twelve

As we approach the Christmas season, we come closer to the supreme symbol of the power of small beginnings. This is a faith that needs to be constantly restored in a world resounding with the loud crash of monstrous machines and organizations—a world, in fact, where "million" sounds like a bit of small change!

There are no Christmas wreaths hung about the following quotation, but it expresses vividly the power of small beginnings. In *Bernard Shaw*, St. John Ervine offers a pungent criticism of H.G. Wells, who violently lectured the Fabian Society on the ground that it was "small and poor"—two unforgiveable sins in the Wells gospel. Mr. Ervine says: "Wells suffered the fatal disease of imagining that big things are better than small ones, and that nothing worth doing can be done by one or two, but only by mobs." He recalls how Mr. Wells, in the spirit of invincible ignorance, bade the "pitiful" little society go out into London's Strand and behold the powers that be: "Note the size of the buildings and business palaces, note the glare of the advertisements, note the abundance of traffic and the multitude of people. . . . How does your little dribble of activities look then?"

Mr. Ervine backs up his case by a powerful little fantasy worth remembering at any season, but particularly at Christmastime. It makes a strong case for anything so little and insignificant as a baby in a barn. Here it is:

If Wells had been a bright young Jew in the middle of the first quarter of the Christian era and had encountered a footsore band of workingmen toiling up the road from Jericho to Jerusalem, he would have addressed them substantially as he addressed the Fabians. One can see him, his fine bright eyes full of laughter, buttonholing Jesus and saying: "My dear chap, what do you and this lot of fishermen and what-nots think you're up to? Use your eyes, man, when you get to Jerusalem. Look at the Roman soldiers in the streets. Go into the temple and take a look at the chief rabbi. See the Romans and the Israelites busy on the well-laid roads . . . . Then ask yourself how you think *you* are going to change all that. My *dear* chap!"

Noel!

Locating the Future

It is hard to locate the future. Any real-estate agent can tell you heartbreaking instances of that, with documentary support. It is as hard to tell in what direction a city will move next as it is to tell what the location of a race horse will be at the end of the race. In the very early days of Washington, D.C.—that city of magnificent distances laid out in the wild, where the streets, in the words of a European visitor, "began nowhere and led nowhere"—there was much speculation about where the city would move. Many operators bet considerable fortunes on its moving west. They lost: it moved east.

Some families in St. Louis have preserved letters written to their ancestors and addressed to "St. Louis, near Alton." The future, obviously, was with Alton, and not with the sleepy town of St. Louis. Perhaps there is an expression of that bad guess about the future in the strangely named railroad, the Chicago & Alton.* Two towns with a great future!

All of which brings us around to Christmas. The most beautiful instance of the location of the future far

---

*Simeon evidently hasn't heard that "the Alton" had become the Gulf, Mobile & Ohio. The first and last seem fairly stable investments, but what would he say about Mobile?—Editor, *The Christian Century*.

from the common expectation is found in the second chapter of Luke, in which the stately roll of the mighty of the time is introduced as a background for the birth of a baby in a barn to a young woman from a town in "the sticks," a girl who would have been called a peasant, or even a "yokel," if Latin had an equivalent for that term of disdain. Hear the pageant roll by: "A decree went out from Caesar Augustus that all the world should be enrolled. This was when Quirinius was governor of Syria." Emperor, governor—just stage props for a baby of unknown family! Of course, the future was with Rome. The boast of heraldry and the pomp of power were all on the side of Rome. But the future was not located in Rome, but in Bethlehem! Incredible, but true. It was one of those "things that cannot be and are."

It has been often pointed out that Clio, the Muse of History, is also the world's greatest jokester. As I remember my mythology—foggily—there was no Muse of Humor, so Clio doubled in both roles. Christmas was her liveliest joke, for the future was not in Rome but in Bethlehem.

Christmas this year comes into a world frantically concerned with the future. Queen Victoria, as a young girl, said to her prime minister, Lord Melbourne, "Don't talk to me about the future, I am bored with it." Our young generation does not feel that way. It is fascinated by the future, sometimes as a bird is fascinated by a deadly snake. Even the kids are intent not on the past of Jason and his Argonauts, but on the tomorrow of Captain Video and his space ship.

It is still hard to locate the future. Will it be in the junk pile and the cemetery? What will be the end of the

Battle of the Centuries as pictured by Carleton S. Coon, in his *The Story of Man*:

Moving out of the Neolithic age may be the world's most difficult problem . . . . It is the retention by Atom Age man of the Neolithic point of view that says, "If your sheep eat our grass we will kill you. We may kill you anyhow to get all the grass for our sheep. Anyone who tries to make us change our ways is a witch and we will kill him."

Does the future, then, belong to the Neolithic Age?
    Christmas comes and sings,

> God rest you merry, gentle folk!
> Let nothing you dismay,

for the future, now as on the first Christmas, is located at Bethlehem.

Star in the Sky

The year 1957 was a year of stars, strange new stars in the sky—stars out of a fantastic dream; Sputnik I and II were chasing each other across the firmament at 18,000 miles an hour. These little stars seemed like portents such as the Roman augurs used to discern in the heavens, terrifying signs of a red doom on the way. Hilltops were crowded with people straining their eyes to catch a glimpse of these new stars disturbing the sky, man-made stars, satellites.

But Christmas brought a reminder greatly needed . . . that there was once another group of people on a hillside looking up at the sky.

> In the bleak midwinter
> Frosty wind made moan,
> Earth stood hard as iron
> Water like a stone.*

A new star appeared then also. "And lo, a star . . . stood over where the young child was"—a new star and a strange one.

> Amid the stars a stranger,
> It beams above a manger.†

*From a poem by Christina G. Rosetti.
†From "The Kings of the East" by Katherine Lee Bates.

But it was not a star of threatening, but of promise and hope. "Star of wonder, star of light." The first words of the Christmas message from the sky were, "Fear not!" "Fear not"—those are good first words for this day of jittery apprehension. Christmas proclaims that "God has not given us a spirit of fear." Christmas brings hope. It ought to turn our minds away from fantastic and fearsome speculations about space and back to earth. Our minds are full of space. Indeed, to hear some people talk you might think that there is nothing in their minds but space, empty space. The most important bit of space is the ground we stand on. "Emanuel" means "God with us," on the earth.

People used to ask eagerly, "Will we get to the moon?" The prior question is, "Will we get to the earth in time to forestall the final explosion and bonfire?" Our big problem is not on the moon but here on earth. It is to continue to weave the fabric of peace, against every obstacle, and to give to that undertaking every energy of mind and heart and sinew.

One of the most direct and passionate pleas for this first concern of the world was made two days after the appearance of the first satellite—not by an evangelistic preacher but in the columns of *The New York Times*. Here it is:

The creature who descended from a tree or crawled out of a cave is now on the eve of incredible journeys. Yet it is not these journeys which chiefly matter. Will we be happier for seeing the other side of the moon, or strolling in the meadows of Mars? The greatest adventure of all is not to go to the moon or to explore the rings of Saturn. It is rather to understand the heart

58

and soul of [humankind], and to turn away from wrath and destruction toward creativeness and love.

A clear echo of an old song which comes across the valley of the centuries: "Peace among people of good will."

> There's a song in the air,
> There's a star in the sky.

And many of them!

Afterword

Reading my father's Christmas pieces once again, most of them for the first time in more than fifteen years, not surprisingly I find them to be sacramental, permitting a burst of light to come through the man Halford Luccock. I discover his character and the meaning of the things he lived by illuminated by what he said about Christmas. Four themes can readily be identified in this writing, leitmotifs, as it were, around which he articulates his testament of Christmas faith.

He perceived first *the irregularity of Christmas*—like roses blooming in the winter. In the first Christmas, he reminds us, everything happened irregularly. How highly inappropriate for the holy birth to happen in a barn! And the memory of that incredible event has ever since "knocked a routine world of order topsy-turvy." And how dull to celebrate it with "appropriate" order and decorum! Rather, he knew "the best gifts of love are those which show a lovely lack of common sense." To read "A Partridge in a Pear Tree" is to sense something of the picaresque Hal Luccock, finding and giving roguish delight in the irregular, the inappropriate, the commonplace, because he saw them as metaphor for transcendent meanings. He was in tune with Annie Dillard, who takes people to task for "making hay when we should be making whoopee." My father made his own whoopee in laughter, play, and sometimes in giving seven yells for the Magnificat. He gave quite a number of loud yells in his lifetime in support of "those of low degree." Many would rise up to call him blessed, because he really believed Christmas was more than "a song in the air"—it was also a "yell in the sanctuary."

Which brings us to the second conspicuous theme— a prophetic discernment of how the light of *Christmas judges the darkness in which we seem content to live.* The wonderful poetry of Christmas opened his eyes to the condemnation of much that seems so important to us. Luccock was a prophet, speaking often in the voice of satire as he imagines how Madison Avenue and the media would have covered "The First Noel" and how the "Wise Men from the West" would have come to Bethlehem. In his own life and in the things he was committed to my father located the future not in Rome or with the wise men from the west, but in Bethlehem.

One can hardly miss a third theme that singularly characterized the man's life: *Christmas offered no place to retire!* He once preached a sermon "Keeping Life Out of Stopping Places." He recognized that Christmas could easily become a beautiful stopping place. But not so for him. The baby grew up. One more reason to get Christmas out of the stocking.

His favorite Christmas story, *A Shepherd* by Heywood Broun, tells of a shepherd who missed the miraculous visitation at Bethlehem because he had to tend a frightened sheep giving birth to a lamb. Asks the eldest shepherd with sarcasm, "Was there for this a great voice out of heaven?" Amos, the lone shepherd, replies, "To my heart, there came a whisper." Hal Luccock heard wonderful whispers at Christmas. And he whispered the wonders to others. Just because the baby grew up, Halford Luccock was always ready to move on from the probable to the wonderful.

He lived on the tiptoe of expectancy because he believed that the good news to all people is not only hope but history. Because "the dayspring from on high hath visited us" he moved with hope to move those great mountains of "prejudice, ignorance, ancestral blindness, entrenched privilege and inertia, which block the road to a better world." Halford Luccock heard and sang the *Christmas music in the key of hope.*

The improbability and wonder of Christmas, the judgment of Bethlehem upon Rome, the hopes that the miracle birth gives to a world in darkness, the journeys to which these hopes call us—four themes he heard in the music of Christmas. Promptings to high and holy laughter, markings of miraculous and gentle joy, an itinerary for the life journey, commencing in hope at Bethlehem—these and others you will find in *A Sprig of Holly.* So, deck the halls with holly!

Robert E. Luccock

Acknowledgments

The publisher wishes to express appreciation for permission to reprint copyrighted essays.

The following articles were published in *The Christian Century* over Halford E. Luccock's pen name, Simeon Stylites: "Christmas Day in the Morning," *The Christian Century,* December 22, 1948; copyright 1948 Christian Century Foundation. "Christmas Meditation," *The Christian Century*, December 21, 1949; copyright 1949 Christian Century Foundation. "A Partridge in a Pear Tree," *The Christian Century,* December 5, 1951; copyright 1951 Christian Century Foundation. "Wise Men from the West," *The Christian Century,* December 10, 1952; copyright 1952 Christian Century Foundation. "Irregular," *The Christian Century,* December 9, 1953; copyright 1953 Christian Century Foundation. "Take Plato Christmas Shopping with You," *The Christian Century,* December 8, 1954; copyright 1954 Christian Century Foundation. "Locating the Future," *The Christian Century,* December 15, 1954; copyright 1954 Christian Century Foundation. "She'll Be Comin' Round the Mountain," *The Christian Century,* December 14, 1955; copyright 1955 Christian Century Foundation. "Let's Give Seven Yells!" *The Christian Century,* February 15, 1956; copyright 1956 Christian Century Foundation. "H.G. Wells Meets the Twelve," *The Christian Century,* December 12, 1956; copyright 1956 Christian